Emily Canada

www.EmilyCanada.com

Written, illustrated & designed
by Emily Canada

Dedication

_____

Baby's Full Name

_____

Born On

_____

Dedicated With Love By

The sweetest flowers
in all the world —
A baby's hands.

– Charles Algernon Swinburne

Table of Contents

Announcing A New Baby

_____

Baby's Full Name

PASTE
BABY
PICTURE
HERE

A baby is an
inestimable blessing !

– Mark Twain

Baby's Origin Story

It All Began With Mom & Dad Falling In Love....

About Mom & Dad

Mom's Full Name

Dad's Full Name

Mom's Birthday

Dad's Birthday

Mom's Birthplace

Dad's Birthplace

Mom's Height

Dad's Height

Mom's Eye Color

Dad's Eye Color

Mom's Hair Color

Dad's Hair Color

Mom's Work

Dad's Work

Mom's Favorite Pastime

Dad's Favorite Pastime

Mom's Favorite Food

Dad's Favorite Food

Mom's Favorite Color

Dad's Favorite Color

Mom's Faith

Dad's Faith

Mom & Dad's Anniversary

Mom & Dad's Song

Mom's Favorite Sport

Dad's Favorite Sport

Mom's Favorite
TV Show

Dad's Favorite
TV Show

Mom's Favorite
Movie / Actor

Dad's Favorite
Movie / Actor

Mom's Favorite
Book / Author

Dad's Favorite
Book / Author

Mom's Favorite
Music / Musician

Dad's Favorite
Music / Musician

Mom's Favorite
Vacation Spot

Dad's Favorite
Vacation Spot

Mom's Age When She Met Dad

Dad's Age When He Met Mom

Hopes & Wishes

Mom & Dad's Hopes & Wishes For Baby

Waiting For Baby

Mom First Knew She Was Pregnant

Baby's Due Date

First Heard Baby's Heartbeat

First Felt Baby Kick

First Saw Baby On The Ultrasound

How Mom & Dad Felt While Waiting For Baby

Sharing The Good News

Who The Good News Was First Shared With

How The Good News Was Celebrated

Who Joined In The Celebration

Best Reactions To The Good News

Baby's Names

Baby's First Name & Meaning

_____

_____

Why We Chose Baby's First Name

_____

_____

_____

_____

Baby's Middle Names And Their Significance

_____

_____

_____

Runner-up First Name & Other First Names Considered

_____

_____

Nicknames

_____

_____

9

Baby's Family Tree

Baby

_____

Brothers & Sisters

_____

Name + Occupation + Birthday + Birthplace

_____

Mom

_____

Aunts

_____

Uncles

_____

Grandma

_____

Grandpa

_____

Great Grandparents

Grandma's Mom

_____

Grandma's Dad

_____

Grandpa's Mom

_____

Grandpa's Dad

_____

Name + Occupation + Birthday + Birthplace

Dad

Aunts

Uncles

Grandma

Grandpa

Great Grandparents

Grandma's Mom

Grandma's Dad

Grandpa's Mom

Grandpa's Dad

Other Family Notables

Great Family Friends

Mom's Baby Shower

Date   Location

Host   Theme

Who + Gift   Who + Gift

Baby Stuff

Some Of The Stuff We Got To Get Ready For Baby

What	What

#CoolBaby

Baby's Coming!

When Mom Went Into Labor

Where Mom Was

What Mom Was Doing

Who Mom Was With

Who Mom Contacted

How Mom Got To The Hospital

Where Dad Was When Mom Went Into Labor

What Dad Was Doing

Who Dad Was With

Who Dad Contacted

How Dad Got To The Hospital

Baby At Birth

Location / Hospital

Date + Day + Time of Birth

Weather
(Circle)   Temp

Who Was In The Delivery Room

Who Was In the Waiting Room

Duration of Labor

Doctor's Name

Mom's First Impressions of Her New Born Baby

Weight

Length

Eye Color

Hair Color

Birthmarks

Features Resemble

Baby Shares Birthday
With These Notable Folks

Dad's First Impression of His New Born Baby

Mom's Delivery Story

_____

_____

_____

_____

_____

_____

_____

_____

_____

_____

Dad's Delivery Story

_____

_____

_____

_____

_____

_____

_____

_____

_____

_____

First Visitors

Date	Who	Relationship To Baby

First Cards & Congratulations

Who	Card / Congratulations

Baby's Footprint

Baby's Handprint

First Day

_____

_____

_____

_____

_____

_____

_____

_____

_____

_____

First Night

_____

_____

_____

_____

_____

_____

_____

_____

_____

_____

Home Sweet Home

Baby Comes Home

Home Address

Color & Theme of Baby's Room

Date Baby Came Home

Who Was There

How Was Baby Greeted

What Was Baby's Mood

Who Visited

Remarks On Dear Baby

Baby's World

*What Was Going On In The World & What
Did Things Cost When Baby Was Born?*

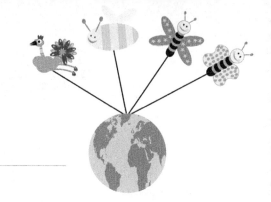

Headline News

President or Prime Minister

Average Life Expectancy

World Population

Country Population

City + Mayor

City Population

Top Songs

Top Bands

Top Movies

Top Actors

Top Books

Top Authors

Top TV Shows

Top TV Personalities

Top Sport Teams

Top Athletes

Top Fashion Trends

Top Models

Average Home Cost	Average Income
Average Apartment Rent	Length of Work Week
Cost of New Car	Cost of a Hamburger
Cost of Gasoline	Cost of Fries
Cost of Milk	Cost of Soda / Pop
Cost of Chocolate Bar	Cost of Chips
Cost of Diapers	Phone Bill
Cost of A Movie Ticket	Heating Bill
Cost of A Cup of Coffee	Power Bill
Cost of Other Things	

Celebrating Baby

Baptism, Bris, Naming Ceremony or Special Celebration

_____

_____

Date
_____

Location
_____

Baby's Outfit
_____

Who Attended
_____

_____

_____

_____

_____

_____

Amazing Baby Moments

Date	Amazing Moment

First Week At Home

Feeding, Sleeping, Happiness, Visitors, Gifts, Mom & Dad's Impressions

Second Week At Home

Feeding, Sleeping, Happiness, Visitors, Gifts, Mom & Dad's Impressions

Bragging About Baby

Baby Is Perfect. Naturally, Mom & Dad Want To List The Ways.

The New Family

Mom & Dad's Thoughts On Their Family & New Baby

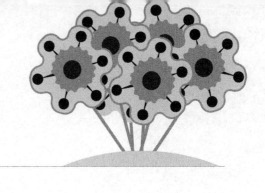

Healthy Baby

Health Information

Blood Type

Allergies

Doctor

Famly Health History

Growing Baby

Stage	Date	Weight	Length
Birth			
Month 1			
Month 2			
Month 3			
Month 4			
Month 5			
Month 6			
Month 7			
Month 8			
Month 9			

Stage	Date	Weight	Length
Month 10			
Month 11			
Month 12			

Thoughts On Baby's Progress

Immunizations

Date	Immunization / Shots	Comments

Illnesses

Start Date	End Date	Health Issue	Notes

Doctor Visits

Date	Health Issue / Checkup	Comments

Date	Health Issue / Checkup	Comments

Notes

Baby's First Year !

1ˢᵗ Month

Things Baby Learned To Do

Sweet Sounds Baby Makes

Best Way To Sooth Baby

Baby Makes Us Laugh When

Songs and Lullabies Baby Likes

How Baby Is Feeding

How Baby Is Sleeping

Thoughts On Baby's 1ˢᵗ Month

2nd Month

Things Baby Learned To Do

Baby's Outings

New Things Baby Likes

Best Way To Sooth Baby

Baby Makes Us Laugh When

How Baby Is Feeding

We Make Baby Smile When

Thoughts On Baby's 2nd Month

3rd Month

EAT SLEEP PLAY!

Things Baby Learned To Do

Sweet Sounds Baby Makes

Baby Makes Us Laugh When

Baby Likes To Cuddle With

New Things Baby Dislikes

Toys Baby Likes

Baby's Visitors

Thoughts On Baby's 3rd Month

4th Month

Things Baby Learned To Do

Best Way To Sooth Baby

We Make Baby Giggle & Laugh When

New Things Baby Likes

Songs & Lullabies Baby Likes

Games & Activities Baby Likes

How Baby Is Feeding

Thoughts On Baby's 4th Month

5th Month

Things Baby Learned To Do

Sweet Sounds Baby Makes

Baby Makes Us Laugh When

We Make Baby Giggle & Laugh When

New Things Baby Dislikes

Toys Baby Likes

How Baby Is Sleeping

Thoughts On Baby's 5th Month

6th Month

B A B Y L O V E S U

Things Baby Learned To Do

Best Way To Sooth Baby

Baby Likes To Cuddle With

New Things Baby Likes

Baby's Outings

Baby's Play Pals

How Baby Is Feeding

Thoughts On Baby's 6th Month

7th Month

Things Baby Learned To Do

Sweet Sounds Baby Makes

Baby Makes Us Laugh When

We Make Baby Giggle & Laugh When

New Things Baby Dislikes

Stories Baby Likes

Toys Baby Likes

Thoughts On Baby's 7th Month

8th Month

Things Baby Learned To Do

Baby Likes To Cuddle With

New Things Baby Likes

Songs & Lullabies Baby Likes

Games & Activities Baby Likes

Baby's Play Pals

How Baby Is Feeding

Thoughts On Baby's 8th Month

9th Month

Things Baby Learned To Do
_____

Sweet Sounds Baby Makes
_____

Baby Makes Us Laugh When
_____

New Things Baby Dislikes
_____

We Make Baby Giggle & Laugh When
_____

Toys Baby Likes
_____

How Baby Is Sleeping
_____

Thoughts On Baby's 9th Month
_____

_____

_____

_____

10th Month

Things Baby Learned To Do

Baby's Sweet Sounds or First Words

Baby Likes To Cuddle With

New Things Baby Likes

Games & Activities Baby Likes

Baby's Outings

How Baby Is Feeding

Thoughts On Baby's 10th Month

11th Month

Things Baby Learned To Do

Baby's Sweet Sounds or First Words

Baby Makes Us Laugh When

We Make Baby Giggle & Laugh When

New Things Baby Dislikes

Toys Baby Likes

How Baby Is Sleeping

Thoughts On Baby's 11th Month

12th Month

Things Baby Learned To Do

Baby's First Words

Baby Likes To Cuddle With

New Things Baby Likes

Stories Baby Likes

Baby's Play Pals

How Baby Is Feeding

Thoughts On Baby's 12th Month

Reflections On Baby's First Year

_____

_____

_____

_____

_____

_____

_____

_____

_____

_____

_____

Fabulous Firsts

Active Baby

First Smile

First Focused Eyes

First Held Up Head

First Rolled Over

First Wave

First Sat Up

First Crawled On Tummy
Or Scooted On Bottom

First Crawled On Hands & Knees

First Stood Up Alone

First Step

First Walk Aided By Furniture

First Unaided Walk

Fun Baby

First Toys

First Playful Noises

First Games

First Parties & Fun Times

First Pets

Superstar Baby

First Photograph

First Video

First Superstar Smile

First Superstar Laugh

First Kiss

First Showed Off To Friends

First Showed Off To Co-Workers

First Big Brag About Baby

First Wave From Baby

First Spoiled Rotten By Grandparents

Other Superstar Moments

Media Savvy Baby

First Lullaby

First Story

First TV Show

First Movie

First Song

Other Media Savvy Moments

Culinary Baby

	Date	Baby's Reaction
First Tried Soft Food		
First Tried Solid Food		
First Used Fingers To Eat		
First Time In High Chair		
First Used Spoon		
First Used Sippy Cup		
First Fruit		
First Vegetables		

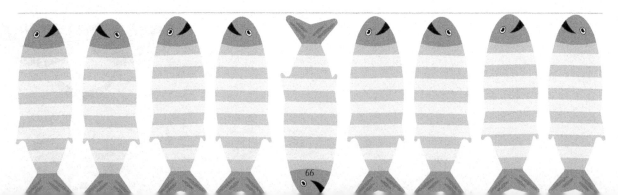

66

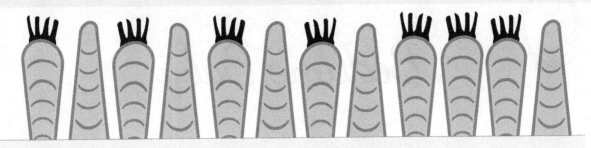

	Date	Baby's Reaction
First Fish		
First Chicken		
First Beef		
First Chocolate		
First Recipe For Baby		

Ingredients + Quantities   How To Prepare

Bedtime Baby

How Many Times Did Baby Fall Asleep and Wake Up First Night At Home

First Time Slept Through The Night

First Crib & Mobile

First Bedtime Snuggle Toy

First Bedtime Story

Bedtime Routines

Bedtime Reflections

Stylish Baby

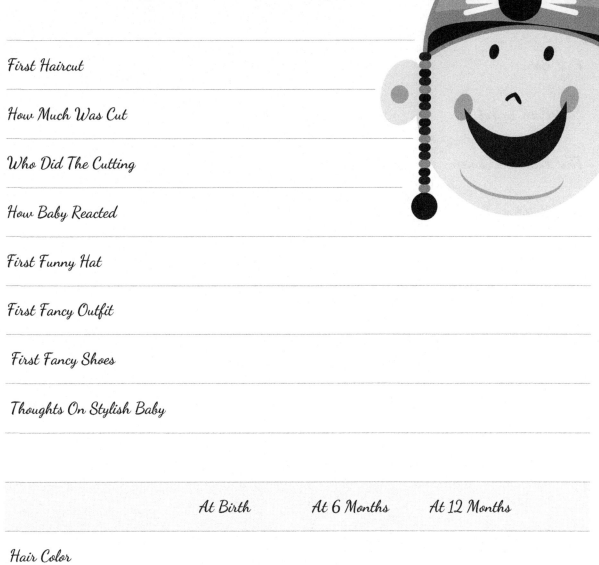

First Haircut

How Much Was Cut

Who Did The Cutting

How Baby Reacted

First Funny Hat

First Fancy Outfit

First Fancy Shoes

Thoughts On Stylish Baby

	At Birth	At 6 Months	At 12 Months
Hair Color			

Bathtime Baby

First Bath

First Bath In Tub

First Bathtime Games

First Bathtime Toy

Mom's Reflections On Bathtime

Well-Traveled Baby

First Outings

First Visits With Family & Friends

First Play Dates & Friends

First Holiday/Vacation Trip

First Time Playing Outdoors / First Park Visit

Chatty Baby

First Cooing

First Babbling

First Word

First Words For Mom

First Words For Dad

Things Baby Could Say By Baby's First Birthday

Baby's First Teeth

Dates   Dates

....

....

....

....

....

....

....

Top

Right   Left

Bottom

First Started Teething   Dentist
_____   _____

Favorite Teething Toy   First Dentist Visit
_____   _____

How Baby Felt About All The Teething
_____

Baby's First Birthday

Party Location

Guests

Gifts

Food Served

Baby's Outfit

Mom's Special Reflections On Baby's First Birthday

Baby's Other Firsts

Make A List Of More Baby Firsts

Reflections On All Of Baby's Fabulous Firsts

Likes & Dislikes

Toys

Month	Likes	Dislikes
1		
2		
3		
4		
5		
6		
7		
8		
9		
10		
11		
12		

And Baby's Award For All Time Favorite Goes To

A

B C

Games

Month	Likes	Dislikes
1		
2		
3		
4		
5		
6		
7		
8		
9		
10		
11		
12		

And Baby's Award For All Time Favorite Goes To

I H E A R T P U P P E T S H O W S

Clothes

Month	Likes	Dislikes
1		
2		
3		
4		
5		
6		
7		
8		
9		
10		
11		
12		

And Baby's Award For All Time Favorite Goes To

Stories & Books

Month	Likes	Dislikes
1		
2		
3		
4		
5		
6		
7		
8		
9		
10		
11		
12		

And Baby's Award For All Time Favorite Goes To

TV Shows
& Movies

Month	Likes	Dislikes
1		
2		
3		
4		
5		
6		
7		
8		
9		
10		
11		
12		

And Baby's Award For All Time Favorite Goes To

Music

Month	Likes	Dislikes
1		
2		
3		
4		
5		
6		
7		
8		
9		
10		
11		
12		

And Baby's Award For All Time Favorite Goes To

Places

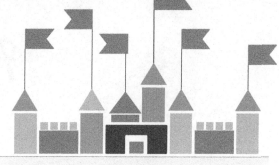

Month	Likes	Dislikes
1		
2		
3		
4		
5		
6		
7		
8		
9		
10		
11		
12		

And Baby's Award For All Time Favorite Goes To

Food

Month	Likes	Dislikes
1		
2		
3		
4		
5		
6		

Month	Likes	Dislikes
7		
8		
9		
10		
11		
12		

And Baby's Award For All Time Favorite Goes To

 # Activities

Month	Likes	Dislikes
1		
2		
3		
4		
5		
6		
7		
8		
9		
10		
11		
12		

And Baby's Award For All Time Favorite Goes To

A Letter To Future Baby

A Letter To Future Baby

Write A Letter For Baby To Read When Baby Is All Grown Up

_____

_____

_____

_____

_____

_____

_____

_____

_____

_____

_____

_____

_____

BABYROCKET

Sign My First Year Book !

Emily Canada

Made in the USA
Monee, IL
06 August 2021